THE YOUNG PERSON'S HISTORY GUIDE TO CANTERBURY

CONTENTS

Eleanor Lynch 3SR.

Written and designed by Martyn Barr
Original illustrations by Rachel Williams
Published by Out of the Box Publishing Limited

This book is dedicated to Chrissie, Alys, Lily and Poppy Barr

Welcome to this brief history guide to Canterbury, the first to be written especially for young people (though I hope adults will enjoy it too!).

Canterbury is one of Britain's oldest and best loved cities. Apart from its world-famous cathedral, the city has many other claims to fame... like having the oldest toilet in England (an achievement not to be sniffed at!).

This history guide doesn't cover everything (that would be a VERY thick book), but I've tried to include all the important events and people over the last 2,000 years or so.

In an historic city like Canterbury the past is all around us and still shapes the way we live, work and travel. The city has been at the forefront of some of the most important events that have taken place in this country, and inspired the people who lived and worked here to go on and do great things. Perhaps you will too!

Martyn Barr

ps. Thank you for buying this book. In doing so you are helping the Demelza House charity care for Kent children who are very ill. Find out more at: www.demelza.org.uk.

IRON MAN

THE CANTIACI OF DUROVERNON

WHAT TO SEE & DO

Bigbury hill fort is now covered by trees. It is located on the Chartham Hatch road, just outside Harbledown.

Archaeological finds from the Iron Age can be seen at the Museum of Canterbury.

DID YOU KNOW...?

Iron Age describes the prehistoric period when cutting tools and weapons were mainly made of iron or steel. It comes after the Stone and Bronze Ages.

The population of Britain during the Iron Age was around one million. Today it is over 60 million.

How did Julius Caesar's attacking armies win the battle of Bigbury? They piled up earth against the fort's defensive banks and climbed over!

This story of Canterbury begins just over 2,000 years ago, towards the end of what we now call the Iron Age. There wasn't much to see of a city then. Durovernon, as it was known by the locals, was just a few simple wooden huts on the swampy banks of the River Stour. It was occupied by Celtic people from northern France called the Belgae, who began to settle in Kent from about 100BC.

Today, Canterbury is surrounded by fields used for grazing animals and growing crops. During the Iron Age, a lot of the area was covered with dense forest, which provided the people with a plentiful supply of wood for building and burning. Being close to an endless supply of clean, fresh water made a lot of sense too; that's why the earliest settlements were often located near rivers, and preferably ones with relatively shallow water, so they could be crossed easily. There were no real roads then, so the River Stour – which was much wider than it is now – was an important route for trade and travel.

Just outside Durovernon at Bigbury, near what is now Harbledown, the Cantiaci tribe built a hill fort. Protected by ditches and a high wooden fence, it was a place of safety for the tribe and the base from which the local chieftain could control his lands.

These early Britons did not write down their history, so archaeologists have had to reconstruct it as best they can from evidence found buried in the ground... and by using their imaginations!

Fortunately, the Roman General Julius Caesar kept detailed records of his many expeditions and battles. He once wrote a description of the local tribespeople of Kent, who must have looked pretty scary: "*All the Britons dye their body with woad, which produces a blue colour and gives them a wild appearance. They wear their hair long; every other part of the body except the upper lip they shave.*"

Although they were always arguing and fighting with neighbouring tribes, the ancient Britons were actually quite a cultured people. Archaeologists have unearthed ornate jewellery, gold, silver, bronze and tin coins and evidence that they were expert potters and weavers.

The year 55BC was probably like most others to the Cantiaci of Durovernon, whose daily routine was largely governed by the cycle of the seasons. But as they quietly went about their everyday lives, little did they know that, just a short distance away across the Channel in Gaul (France), Julius Caesar and his armies were preparing to invade and take over their lands!

1. Gold torc, a Celtic symbol of power and strength, worn around the neck, waist, arm or chest

2. Artist's impression of the Iron Age settlement of Durovernon, based on archaeological remains

3. Iron Age gold coin known as a stater, found with others near Chartham Hatch

4. Reconstruction of an Iron Age boat, made from a single hollowed out tree trunk

5. Bigbury hill fort today, hidden beneath woodland overlooking Harbledown

1. Artist's impression of Roman Durovernum, based on archaeological remains – the impressive theatre (centre) is located in what is now St Margaret's Street

2. Roman glass bottle containing a person's cremated remains

3. Hoard of Roman coins: each denomination can be distinguished by its metal, size, weight and sometimes by the emperor's headdress!

4. Reconstruction of a first century Roman Optio in full battle armour – equivalent to today's second-in-command or Lieutenant

5. Statue of the most famous Roman General of them all: Julius Caesar

BATH TIME
ROMANS RULE BRITANNIA!

By this time, Romans occupied most of continental Europe. Having recently conquered the Gauls in France, Julius Caesar now set his sights on the white-cliffed island that he could see across the Channel.

He had heard many reports from traders that 'Britannia' was a rich source of minerals and metals, which he needed to make swords, armour and chariots for his armies. He was also told that the farmland in the south of Britain produced an abundance of corn, the staple diet for hungry Roman legions. Caesar was confident that the uncivilised Britons would be no match for his heavily armed and well disciplined soldiers. How wrong he was!

On 25 August in 55BC Julius Caesar set sail for the Kent coast with over 10,000 men in 80 ships. He landed near Deal but a heavy storm prevented all his cavalry troops from getting ashore and many of his ships were smashed to pieces on the beach. Caesar's invasion force immediately met with fierce resistance from the local people and their awesome war chariots. But eventually the Britons were overpowered and pleaded for peace. Taking hostages, Julius Caesar returned to Gaul for the winter.

The following spring he mounted another attack. This time, with a 30,000-strong army, he made it further inland and managed to conquer Bigbury hill fort and overpower the local tribal leader, Cassivellaunus. In order to get rid of Caesar and his army, Cassivellaunus agreed to pay large sums of money to the Romans. But he never did and, despite this, the tribe was left alone for nearly a hundred years.

In 43AD the Roman General Aulus Plautius landed on the Kent coast at Richborough under strict orders from Emperor Claudius to conquer Britain once and for all. The Britons again put up a brave fight, but this time the invasion force of more than 40,000 soldiers triumphed. After a series of bloody battles over many years, Britain too became a Roman colony.

The Romans chose a site by the River Stour crossing for their new town, Durovernum Cantiacorum, which in Latin means 'the marshy, alder-grove of the Cantiaci'. They shared the town with the local Belgic tribe and eventually established a military base there. Over the course of the next hundred years or so, the Romans cleared the ground, laid out gravel streets in

WHAT TO SEE & DO

The Canterbury Roman Museum – located underground at the level of the Roman town – is an exciting mix of excavated real objects, reconstructions and the remains of a Roman town house. You can also see some Roman finds at the Museum of Canterbury.

The Roman bastion display can be found by the city wall near the bus station. The bastion – or defensive tower – was discovered during the archaeological dig at Whitefriars.

A small part of the Roman Quenin Gate is visible in the city wall in the Broad Street car park. See if you can find it!

You can see a section of the original Roman city wall in St Radigunds Street on the outside of the former St Mary's Church.

5

a grid pattern and erected a series of impressive public buildings, including a theatre, town hall, temple, forum and bathhouses. Plots of land were sold so people could build Roman-style houses. Straight Roman roads were constructed to link Durovernum with Londinium (London) and the Roman coastal ports of Dubris (Dover), Rutupiae (Richborough) and Lemanis (Lympne). Many of these major routes still exist today.

The appeal of the new Roman town grew. Settlers arrived from other parts of the Roman empire. Wealthy local people built themselves houses in Durovernum. Roman soldiers and officials stopped off on their way to other towns, or back to Rome. The now thriving town attracted traders, craftsmen and shopkeepers.

Gradually the local people grew to like the Roman way of life. Some Romans married Britons and had families and eventually the two peoples became one: the Romano-British.

FOCUS ON: ROMAN LIFE

Most people in Roman Canterbury lived in single storey houses. Often the front room was used as a shop or workshop, opening out directly on to the street. Richer people could afford to have their floors covered in elaborate mosaics.

Most homes were heated by small charcoal burners; larger houses had underfloor heating systems known as hypocausts. The majority of houses had small gardens where people could grow their own fruit and vegetables.

Roman men in Canterbury wore a simple tunic, which also doubled up as a nightshirt. They might wear a toga over the top if on official business and, in cold weather, a cloak. Roman ladies took great care over their appearance and were keen to keep up with all the latest fashions from Rome... just like today! A Roman lady would wear an ankle-length tunic covered by a shorter one or a mini toga. The colour of her dress would denote her position in society, as would her jewellery. Her hairstyle and make-up would be very elaborate.

ROMAN DINNER MENU

STARTERS
OYSTERS, MUSSELS, SNAILS FATTENED ON MILK, ENDIVE & RADISH SALAD

MAIN COURSE
BOILED HAM WITH HONEY BAKED IN PASTRY, ROAST PEACOCK SERVED WITH A SPICED SAUCE, ROAST SUCKLING PIG, STUFFED DORMICE, ASPARAGUS, CABBAGE, PARSNIPS AND TURNIPS

DESSERT
PLUMS, CHERRIES, QUINCES, POMEGRANATES, GRAPES, AND PASTRY CASES FILLED WITH HONEY, RAISINS, DATES AND NUTS
BORDEAUX WINE

The main meal of the day was eaten in the evening off low tables whilst reclining on sofas. Diners used spoons and knives but no forks... and eating with your fingers was considered perfectly acceptable! Wealthy Romans enjoyed a varied diet of meat, fish, vegetables and fruit, washed down with wines from Italy, Spain, France and Germany. Poorer people made do with beer brewed from locally grown barley.

The Romans worshipped many gods, with Jupiter as their chief, and every home had a little shrine to the family's own household god. Sometimes emperors were also worshipped, with temples built in their honour. Christianity began in the Roman empire. Followers were initially persecuted for their beliefs, then allowed to practise their religion freely. Finally, in 313AD, Christianity became the official Roman religion.

Romans took their cleanliness very seriously and every town, including Durovernum, had its own bath house. After changing out of their toga, Romans would jump into a cold pool before passing through a series of hot, warm and cold rooms. Along the way, oil was rubbed over their bodies. The oil (and dirt!) was removed with a blunt scraper called a strigil. A warm water rinse was followed by another cold plunge and perhaps a massage.

A visit to the baths was not only a pleasurable experience but also an essential part of a Roman man's regular routine, with plenty of time to meet up with friends, gamble, gossip and discuss business.

When a Roman died, his or her body was cremated. The ashes were placed in an urn and buried in a cemetery outside the town walls, along with some personal possessions. Later in the Roman period, bodies were buried in coffins in individual graves.

① Artist's impression of Anglo-Saxon Cantwaraburh, based on archaeological remains: the once magnificent Roman town lies in ruins

② St Martin's Church in Canterbury – the oldest parish church in England still in use and the base for St Augustine's mission to Kent

③ The Anglo-Saxon Canterbury cross, discovered in St George's Street in 1867, has been a symbol for the city and cathedral since Victorian times

④ Bronze statue of King Ethelbert, one of Kent's most powerful Anglo-Saxon kings

⑤ Jewellery like this was popular in the seventh century: this mount probably came from a larger pendant necklace

RAIDERS AND SETTLERS
ANGLO-SAXONS CONQUER KENT

During the third century, raiders from continental Europe began attacking Kent, so a 10m high stone wall was built around Durovernum, along with a series of fortified gates. This circuit of walls established by the Romans still exists, but today's town walls are mostly Medieval in origin.

Over the next hundred years, the raids increased. Other parts of the Roman empire were being attacked and many Roman soldiers were ordered to leave Britain. In 410 the Romans left Durovernum for good, taking with them the Christian religion, their civic pride and their brick-making skills. It would be many years before all three would return.

Without protection from the Romans, the town was vulnerable to attack from raiders. Nobody knows for sure what happened to the Romano-British residents of Durovernum. They may have simply abandoned the town and set up homes in the surrounding countryside. We do know that the once magnificent Roman town fell into ruin.

Archaeologists have discovered a thick layer of black soil which dates from this time: the remains of grass, weeds and trees that took over when there was no-one left to look after the roads and buildings.

Eventually, some of the newcomers decided to set up home there. First came pagan tribes of Saxons from North Germany and Holland and Angles and Jutes from Denmark. We use one name to describe all these groups: Anglo-Saxons.

No-one is really sure why the Anglo-Saxons came to this country. It may have been because their land often flooded. It was difficult to grow crops, so they were looking for new places to settle down and farm. Some say that Saxon warriors were invited to come to Britain.

The Anglo-Saxons built wooden houses with wattle and daub walls, earth floors and thatched roofs within the Roman walls. Later they began to build in stone, often using bricks and stones from the crumbling Roman buildings.

There were many battles as more and more settlers arrived. One of the Jutish raiding parties was led by two brothers, Hengist and Horsa. At first they offered to help the local people defend themselves against more raiders. But it was a trick and they conquered Kent.

By the end of the 6th century the Anglo-Saxons controlled most of southern Britain, which they began to call 'Angleland'. The town's name changed again... to Cantwaraburh (the fortified town of the men of Kent)!

DID YOU KNOW...?

Most Anglo-Saxons were either freemen or slaves. A freeman owned land and slaves. A slave owned nothing and was the freeman's property.

Slaves were sometimes buried with their masters, so that they could carry on serving them in the afterlife!

Richer freemen were known as 'thanes'. The most important thanes helped the king rule.

The Anglo-Saxons didn't have prisons. For minor crimes, a nose or a hand might be cut off. If a person killed someone they had to pay money to the dead person's relatives.

King Alfred (849-899) decided that a book should be written about the Anglo-Saxons. It was called the *Anglo-Saxon Chronicle*. Much of what we know about the Anglo-Saxons comes from this book.

5

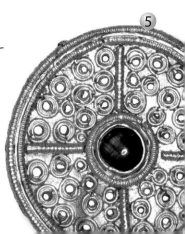

MAN WITH A MISSION

AUGUSTINE THE EVANGELIST

WHAT TO SEE & DO

You can explore the ruins of St Augustine's Abbey, now part of Canterbury's World Heritage Site. There's a fascinating museum and free audio tour included in the admission price.

Bronze statues of King Ethelbert and Queen Bertha have been erected on Lady Wootton's Green.

In time, things began to settle down in Anglo-Saxon Cantwaraburh. A new town became established and craftsmen, farmers and merchants began to trade again. By now England was divided into a number of separate kingdoms, each ruled by a king.

In 597 Pope Gregory sent Augustine and a group of 40 monks from Rome on a mission to restore the Christian religion to southern England. Augustine planned to convert the Royal families first, hoping that the people would follow their example.

Kent was a good starting point. Not only was it the closest kingdom to the Continent, but it was ruled by Ethelbert, one of the most powerful of all the kings. His wife Bertha, who was from France, was already a Christian. She worshipped at St Martin's Church just outside the city walls, and not far from her royal palace.

King Ethelbert welcomed the missionaries. He gave them somewhere to live and allowed them to preach freely to the people. Before long he became a Christian. He gave Augustine an old Roman church in the town, which was to become the cathedral, and a site not far away to establish a monastery.

The new monastery – or abbey – was home to Augustine and the monks who had accompanied him from Italy. It would also become the burial site for the Kentish kings and early archbishops of Canterbury. The original abbey, which was headed by an abbot, would have housed a dining hall, a dormitory and a series of chapels for worship. Much of the remains of this first abbey lie buried beneath later monastic buildings built on the site.

The first six abbots were all Italian, either from the initial band of missionaries who had arrived with Augustine, or from a new group sent by the Pope in 601 to help

①

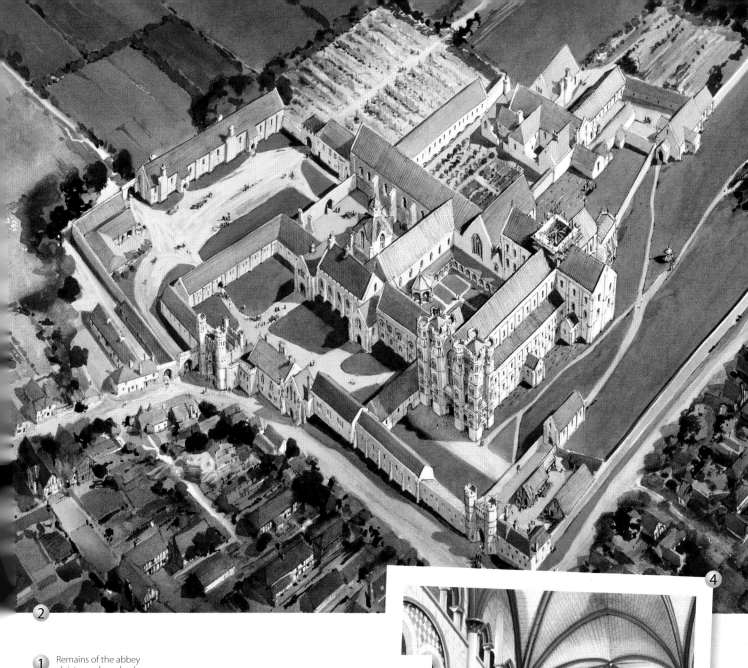

2

4

3

1 Remains of the abbey cloister and royal palace of King Henry VIII

2 Artist's impression of St Augustine's Abbey around 1500

3 Artist's impression of the cloister after it was rebuilt in the 13th century

4 Artist's impression of the nave of the huge abbey church, looking east

5 (Overleaf) Remains of the crypt – this was below the church's high altar and was used for worship and burials

spread the gospel. The monks based their lives on the Rule of St Benedict, so they were known as Benedictines.

At this time, monasteries were the only places for higher education in England. In the seventh century the church school in Cantwaraburh was famous for its teaching and attracted students from all over the country. Subjects taught included scripture, poetry, law, calligraphy, astronomy, music and medicine. The monks produced beautiful 'illuminated' manuscripts and the monastery soon built up a large library.

Abbeys were expected to be self-sufficient and for that they needed land. In the early days monks did a lot of the manual work themselves but then they hired servants to do the job for them, and that required more money! The land close to the abbey was probably given by King Ethelbert, and large areas in Thanet were

given by the Viking King Cnut (more about him later!). Rich people often paid monks money or gave them land to say prayers for them. At its height, St Augustine's, as the abbey became known, owned about 12,000 acres of land... equivalent to nearly 7,000 football pitches!

After the Norman conquest in 1066, William the Conqueror wanted to reinforce his claim to the English throne by rewarding his supporters with land and titles. He appointed his choice of people to important positions and encouraged the building of new monasteries and the rebuilding of existing ones.

William appointed Italian monk Lanfranc as Archbishop of Canterbury and French monk Scolland as Abbot of St Augustine's. Abbot Scolland undertook a survey of the abbey buildings. He was worried that the place was so old that it might collapse, so he asked the Pope's permission to rebuild the abbey. Work began almost immediately and over the next 30 years or so a huge new abbey church was built. It rivalled the cathedral in its size and magnificence! In time the monks' living quarters were also replaced.

Over the next few hundred years, more additions were made. Part of the church had to be rebuilt after a fire in 1168 and an earthquake in 1382 led to more repairs and the upgrading of several buildings. During the 15th century building work finally slowed down... quite possibly because the abbey had run out of money!

5

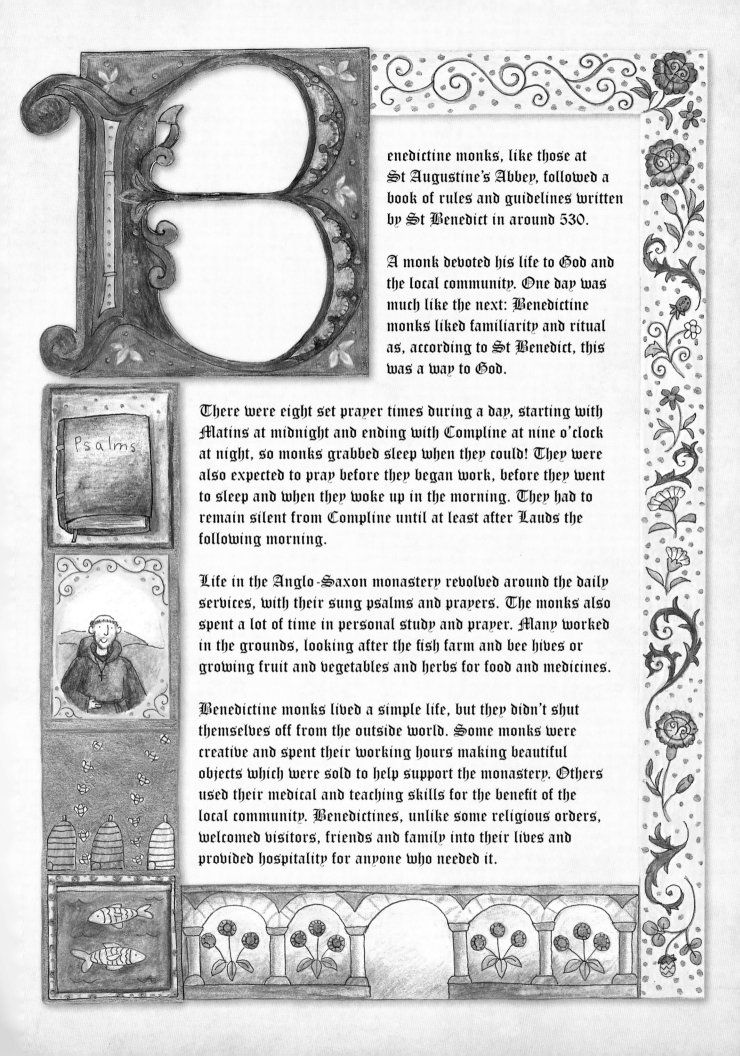

Benedictine monks, like those at St Augustine's Abbey, followed a book of rules and guidelines written by St Benedict in around 530.

A monk devoted his life to God and the local community. One day was much like the next: Benedictine monks liked familiarity and ritual as, according to St Benedict, this was a way to God.

There were eight set prayer times during a day, starting with Matins at midnight and ending with Compline at nine o'clock at night, so monks grabbed sleep when they could! They were also expected to pray before they began work, before they went to sleep and when they woke up in the morning. They had to remain silent from Compline until at least after Lauds the following morning.

Life in the Anglo-Saxon monastery revolved around the daily services, with their sung psalms and prayers. The monks also spent a lot of time in personal study and prayer. Many worked in the grounds, looking after the fish farm and bee hives or growing fruit and vegetables and herbs for food and medicines.

Benedictine monks lived a simple life, but they didn't shut themselves off from the outside world. Some monks were creative and spent their working hours making beautiful objects which were sold to help support the monastery. Others used their medical and teaching skills for the benefit of the local community. Benedictines, unlike some religious orders, welcomed visitors, friends and family into their lives and provided hospitality for anyone who needed it.

1. Reconstruction of a typical Viking port

2. A longship is set on fire as part of the traditional Up Helly Aa Viking festival, celebrating the coming of another year

3. Viking knife made from iron with a carved bone handle – found on a dig in Castle Street, Canterbury

4. Written in the Viking alphabet or runes, these stones were erected as memorials to the dead

5. The name of a Viking longship was reflected in the shape of its prow: 'Long Serpent', 'Snake of the Sea' and 'Horse of the Home of Ice' were popular choices

VICIOUS VIKINGS
SIEGE AND SEIZURE

During the 9th and 10th centuries, Viking raids threatened the peace and stability of Cantwaraburh.

The Vikings came from three countries in Scandinavia: Denmark, Norway and Sweden. They were also known as the Norse people. Vikings may have been fierce warriors but they were mostly farmers, or worked as craftsmen or traders.

Cantwaraburh survived two waves of attacks from the Vikings between 835 and 855, and from 991 to 1012, but 'great slaughter' was witnessed in the town in 842.

The Vikings demanded increasingly large sums of money called Danegeld to make them go away. In 1009 the people of Kent paid £3,000 to Thorkell to leave them in peace, but two years later he and his bloodthirsty band returned, this time demanding the cathedral treasures.

Canterbury's citizens defended the town for nearly three weeks before the Vikings finally broke in, setting fire to the cathedral and most of the houses. Many people were killed and Alphege – the Archbishop of Canterbury – and other church leaders were taken hostage. Alphege pleaded with the townspeople not to pay a ransom for him and, later, was killed with oxbones at a drunken feast at Greenwich in London. He was named a saint for his brave and selfless act.

After more bloody battles, one of the Viking chiefs, Cnut, was crowned King of England. As a sign of remorse for what had happened to Alphege, he returned the body of the murdered archbishop to the cathedral in 1023, where it was placed in an elaborate shrine. He also handed over the treasured remains of St Mildred – St Mildred's Church was built in gratitude – and gave many rich gifts and land to the church.

When King Harold was beaten by William the Conqueror at the Battle of Hastings in 1066, it marked the end of Viking rule in England. Meanwhile, in Scotland, powerful Viking earls continued to control the islands and some of the mainland for hundreds of years.

William's succession to the English throne was the start of an exciting new chapter in this country's – and Canterbury's – history. Many of the great cathedrals, churches and castles built in Norman times can still be seen today... including the 'big church' at the heart of the city: Canterbury Cathedral.

WHAT TO SEE & DO

Archbishop Alphege's murder is commemorated in a stained-glass window in the cathedral. See if you can find it!

DID YOU KNOW...?

The name 'Viking' comes from Old Norse. It means 'a pirate raid'.

Viking children did not go to school. They helped their parents at work, and learned about history, religion and the law from stories. They became adults at the age of 15 or 16.

Thor was the most popular Viking god. He ruled the skies, storms and thunder. He had iron gloves, a magic belt and a giant hammer! Thursday is named after him.

5

UNDER CONSTRUCTION

THE GREAT CATHEDRAL BUILDERS

WHAT TO SEE & DO

Canterbury Cathedral is open most days of the year though may be closed at times for services and special events. There is an admission charge but you may qualify for a free pass.

DID YOU KNOW...?

Canterbury Castle was built in 1080 and is one of only three Royal castles in Kent. During the 19th century it was used to store coal!

Mint Yard near the Green Court had nothing to do with peppermints. It was where coins were made or 'minted'.

① A tin-lead token of the tomb of St Thomas Becket: a souvenir for a pilgrim to take home!

Augustine's original cathedral was rebuilt and enlarged by the Anglo-Saxons, but it was destroyed by fire just after the Norman conquest. Between 1070 and 1077 the first Norman Archbishop of Canterbury, Lanfranc, rebuilt it, together with a priory alongside to house 150 Benedictine monks. He took many of his design ideas from the cathedral he had built at Caen in France, and from where most of the stone for the building came.

Constructing such a colossal building and transporting huge lumps of stone from France was no mean feat! Roads then were just muddy, bumpy tracks. The solution was to bring the stone as far as possible by river and sea on barges. The stone was off-loaded on to wooden carts at Fordwich. When you look at the small village today, it's hard to imagine that this was once a bustling port for Canterbury!

The building of the new cathedral, combined with the rebuilding works at St Augustine's Abbey, meant that there were plenty of jobs for builders, carpenters, stonemasons and other craftsmen. Once again Canterbury enjoyed a revival in its fortunes.

After Thomas Becket's murder in 1170 his shrine became one of the most important places of pilgrimage outside the Holy Land. As many as 100,000 pilgrims travelled to Becket's shrine every year from all over Europe.

In those days, roofs were often just made of wood or thatch and, with buildings lit by candles, there was always the danger of fire. In 1174, disaster struck and fire destroyed part of Lanfranc's great cathedral. The famous Norman architect William of Sens was given the job of rebuilding it. One day whilst working he slipped and fell off the wooden scaffolding and was badly injured. Another William took his place: William the Englishman, who eventually finished the work.

A staircase and a few walls are all that remain today of Lanfranc's original Norman cathedral. Over the next few centuries, new parts were added and existing ones changed. The Norman nave, built in the 'Romanesque' style, was replaced in the 14th century by Henry Yevele, the King's master mason.

The Bell Harry Tower – at 72m the highest landmark in Canterbury – was completed in 1498. The building of one of the most magnificent cathedrals this country has ever seen was finally completed!

FOCUS ON: CANTERBURY CATHEDRAL

The Chapter House is the largest of its kind in England. The monks met there to discuss the cathedral's business. They studied and talked together outside in the cloisters, sitting on stone benches that have been worn smooth by centuries of bottoms!

The inside of the cathedral was once brightly painted, with colourful pictures on the walls. These have faded in time or were removed in the 17th century by the Puritans, who believed that churches should be very plain.

As you walk around the outside of the cathedral look out for 'grotesques', comical figures carved out of stone. Their strange contorted faces are supposed to frighten away evil spirits!

There's some very old graffiti on the crypt walls! Was it carved by the stonemasons, pilgrims or maybe mischievous monks?

Monks used to have one bath a year but had to wash before every prayer time. This required a regular supply of clean water. Abbot Wilbert solved the problem in the 12th century by laying pipes fed by five springs from outside the town walls to a water tank in the cathedral.

The Corona Chapel was built to house the top (or crown) of St Thomas' head, which was cut off when he was murdered.

The cathedral quire – where the monks sang their daily prayers – was the first 'Gothic' building in England. It included 'flying buttresses' on the outside to support the walls and ceilings, which meant you could build a lot higher.

Some of the cathedral's stained-glassed windows are known as the 'Bible of the poor'. Many people could not read, so these windows helped them understand the Bible stories.

The cathedral has 21 bells in total. Only one is housed in the tallest tower: Bell Harry, which is used to call people to services. It is also rung to mark the death of a king, queen or archbishop.

REST IN PEACE

NOSEY PARKER

Henry IV is the only English king to be buried in Canterbury Cathedral. Edward the Black Prince, who died in 1376, asked to be buried in the crypt but was thought to be so important that his tomb was placed near to that of St Thomas. When the chapel containing the tomb of Archbishop Stephen Langton was rebuilt to make way for wealthy Lady Holland's, his was pushed so far back that his feet stick out into the yard outside! Archbishop Matthew Parker upset a lot of people by poking his nose in to their business while hunting down historic documents. They nicknamed him Nosey Parker, a term we still use today!

1. Artist's impression of Medieval Canterbury

2. Stained glass window in the cathedral commemorating St Thomas Becket

3. Look up into Bell Harry tower to see this stunning fan vaulting!

4. Altar of the Sword's Point, marking the spot where St Thomas Becket was brutally murdered

5. Illustration in the *Life of St Thomas Becket* published in Canterbury around 1180

FOCUS ON: ST THOMAS BECKET

The murder of Archbishop Thomas Becket in the cathedral in 1170 is probably the best known event in Canterbury's history.

In 1154 King Henry II made Thomas his Chancellor, the most powerful official in the kingdom. Thomas certainly had the right skills and experience for the job. He had distinguished himself in battle, was well educated and loved expensive clothes and food. You always knew when Chancellor Becket was in town by the colourful and noisy procession that went before him!

Henry and Thomas were both strong-willed characters but they soon became good friends. When Archbishop Theobald died in 1162 King Henry named Thomas as his successor, thinking that it would be a good idea to have *his* man on the inside, so that he could reduce the power of the church. But Thomas took his new priestly role very seriously and always sided with the church against the king.

Thomas chose to live a simple monastic life, perhaps to make up for all his excesses whilst Chancellor. He no longer wore lavish clothes and jewellery but a simple monk's habit over a horse hair shirt, which quickly became infested with lice and fleas. He slept on a cold stone floor and every morning would wash the feet of 13 poor people, feed them and give them money.

King Henry had expected Thomas' full support, but they were always arguing. Things got so bad at one point that the king banished Thomas to France. The final straw came when Thomas

excommunicated some of his fellow church leaders for siding with Henry. That meant they could no longer be members of the church, a very serious punishment indeed. When the king heard this he became extremely angry and exclaimed: "*Who will rid me of this turbulent priest?*" His outburst was overheard by four Norman knights: Richard Brito, Hugh de Moreville, Reginald FitzUrse and William de Tracy, who pledged to do something about it.

On the evening of 29 December 1170, the four knights confronted Thomas at his house in Palace Street. The frightened monks tried desperately to persuade Thomas to seek sanctuary in the cathedral, but he only did so when he heard Vespers being sung, requiring his attendance. The knights followed Thomas and found him kneeling at the altar and demanded that he pardon the men he had excommunicated. Thomas refused and told the knights that "*for the name of Jesus and the protection of the church, I am ready to embrace death.*"

Seething with anger, the knights struck Thomas three times, the last blow so hard that the sword blade snapped in two. One blow sliced off the top of Thomas' head and his blood and brains spilled on to the stone floor.

Shortly after his violent death, a series of miracles were reported and Thomas was declared a saint by Pope Alexander III three years later. Pilgrims soon began to flock to his shrine in the cathedral. One of them was the king himself, dressed in sackcloth and walking barefoot, repenting for the terrible deed he had caused to happen.

FOCUS ON: THE CANTERBURY TALES

The Canterbury Tales is the most famous work of Geoffrey Chaucer, a 14th century English writer and poet. It tells the story of a group of pilgrims who meet at the Tabard Inn in Southwark, London, before setting out on a pilgrimage to Canterbury to visit St Thomas Becket's tomb.

The pilgrims come from all walks of life. There are religious characters such as a prioress, monk and a pardoner, as well as a shipman, miller, carpenter, reeve, squire, yeoman and a knight. Inn keeper Harry Bailey suggests a game where they tell stories to each other along the way. The pilgrims agree to tell four stories each, two on the way to Canterbury and two on the way back. The person who, in Harry's opinion, tells the best story will have his supper paid for by the rest of the group.

First to speak is the knight, then each person tells a story that reflects their position in life. Some tell stories that make fun of others in the group; others are funny, serious or very rude! In the end, no winner is chosen, and not all of the pilgrims have told their tales by the time the story ends. In fact, the pilgrims don't even reach Canterbury!

This rather incomplete ending is a bit of a mystery. It may be that Chaucer died before he could change or finish the book. William Caxton, England's first printer, published *The Canterbury Tales* in the 1470s, and the book is still sold today.

Chaucer's style of writing was revolutionary at the time and he is often referred to as the 'Father of English literature'.

TALL TALES AND TOURISTS
A PLACE OF PILGRIMAGE

The popularity of Canterbury as a pilgrim destination attracted people from all over Europe. Goldsmiths, mercers, weavers, tanners, smiths, shoemakers and dyers all worked in the town and parts of Canterbury became known for the specific trades that were located there.

The church continued to prosper. In addition to the cathedral and its priory, St Gregory's Priory (also founded by Lanfranc) and St Augustine's Abbey, there were 22 other churches in the town. The wealth of the church was boosted by large sums of money paid by pilgrims visiting the shrine of St Thomas, around whom a whole new tourist industry grew. In those days, saints and martyrs were equivalent to today's pop idols and were 'worshipped' just as enthusiastically!

Pilgrimage to holy places was an important part of Medieval life and pilgrims loved to take home souvenirs of their visit. Many people had travelled a long way, so they needed places to stay and rest. The most famous pilgrim inn at the time was located close to the cathedral in Mercery Lane. It was called the Cheker of Hope.

Some pilgrims couldn't afford to stay at inns, so free accommodation was provided for them at places like Eastbridge Hospital (which comes from the word for hospitality rather than somewhere you go when you are ill!).

Canterbury's popularity also attracted other religious groups. Named after the colour of their robes or 'habits', Black, Grey and White Friars began to set up their own religious houses from about 1200. Whilst monks and priests devoted themselves to prayer and study, friars saw their spiritual role as ministering to the needs of others, by preaching and tending the poor and sick.

By the middle of the 14th century, Canterbury was one of the most densely populated towns in England, with some 10,000 residents. Within less than 200 years, this number had dropped to just 3,000 – the result of plagues and other deadly diseases, many of which are perfectly treatable today.

WHAT TO SEE & DO

Step back to the Middle Ages at the Canterbury Tales visitor attraction and join the pilgrims on their journey from London to Canterbury.

Eastbridge Hospital in the High Street has sheltered pilgrims, soldiers, school boys and now elderly people for over 800 years.

Hidden away behind Stour Street is a 13th century building over the River Stour. It's the oldest Franciscan building in Britain and all that remains of Greyfriars Friary.

Check out Medieval poo under the microscope at the Museum of Canterbury!

DID YOU KNOW...?

St John's Hospital in Northgate is home to England's oldest toilet. It has been used for over 900 years. Men and women sat on separate toilet seats, but in the same room!

The water from the pump in Palace Street came out a pink colour as it passed through iron pipes. It was sold to pilgrims who were told it contained a drop of St Thomas Becket's blood!

 Canterbury pilgrims leaving the city, from a manuscript published around 1460

TUDOR TANTRUMS

THE DISSOLUTION OF THE MONASTERIES

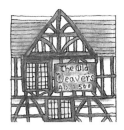

WHAT TO SEE & DO

Take a river boat tour from behind The Weavers in St Peter's Street. It's a great way to see places you may never have seen before!

St Dunstan's Church is 1,000 years old and the first to be dedicated to the saint. It is said to be the final resting place of Sir Thomas More's head!

Elizabeth I visited Canterbury in 1573 and 'entertained' the Duke of Alençon in what is now known as Queen Elizabeth's Guest Chamber in the High Street.

By the start of the 16th century people were becoming increasingly critical of the wealth and power of the church. Ordinary people had every right to complain, as monks and priests often lived lives of luxury compared with theirs. Many, too, seem to have forgotten the solemn vows they made about living a pure and holy life!

Like his predecessors, King Henry VIII wanted to reduce the church's power in England, as well as raise money to finance his expensive wars against France and Scotland. Finally, when the Pope refused to grant him a divorce from Catherine of Aragon, Henry retaliated by establishing his own church – the Church of England – declaring himself its Supreme Head. In doing so, Henry set off a process in this country known as the Reformation, when England stopped being a Roman Catholic country and became Protestant.

In 1536 Henry ordered the closing down of all the abbeys, monasteries and convents across England, Wales and Ireland. This 'Dissolution' took four years to complete. Henry kept a lot of the wealth for himself and distributed the rest amongst his friends and favourite officials. Many monastic buildings were destroyed and their stone and bricks used to build impressive houses for the new land owners.

The Dissolution had a dramatic effect on Canterbury. The shrine of St Thomas was destroyed and St Augustine's Abbey and all its lands and properties were handed over to the king. Henry built a royal palace there for himself and his new wife, Anne of Cleves (number four!).

The cathedral priory was closed down, but the cathedral itself was allowed to carry on as an Anglican church, the 'Mother Church of the Anglican Communion'.

Many of the former priory buildings were taken over by the cathedral or by the re-established priory school. By a royal charter of 1541 this became known as The King's School. With Canterbury's popular visitor attraction shut down you may think this would lead to a decline in the town's fortunes. But like so many other periods in its colourful 2,000-year history, Canterbury bounced back, and the next 150 years were just as dramatic and colourful as the previous.

Before long, Henry had created a new reason for pilgrimage. People who annoyed or disobeyed the king often found their heads on the chopping block (perhaps that's where we get the

1. Gold medal with the Latin inscription: 'Henry VIII, King of England, France and Ireland, defender of the faith, and under Christ, the supreme head on earth of the Church of England and Ireland'

2. Artist's impression of Tudor Canterbury

3. King Henry VIII, as pictured in a 19th century engraving

4. The execution of Archbishop of Canterbury, Thomas Cranmer, taken from the *Book of Martyrs, Actes and Monuments* published in 1563

5. Queen Elizabeth's Guest Chamber in Canterbury High Street

6. (Overleaf) The Weavers, one of the most photographed of Canterbury's buildings, was used to house weavers who had fled religious persecution in Europe

DID YOU KNOW...?

Butchery Lane was home to... the town's butchers! See if you can spot the bull on the wall!

Buttermarket used to be called 'Bullstake'. Bulls were tied up here and dogs allowed to attack them, both for 'fun' and because it was believed that it made the flesh more tender.

An easy way to remember Henry VIII's wives: divorced, beheaded, died, divorced beheaded, survived!

Jelly was a very popular Tudor dessert, as sugar was very expensive at the time. If you could afford jelly you were considered to be very rich!

Henry VIII was so rich that he refused to wipe his own bottom. He employed someone to do it for him who was known as the Groom of the Stool!

term 'blockhead'?). His Chancellor, Sir Thomas More, refused to swear an oath declaring Henry to be the head of the Church of England. As a result, Thomas lost his, which Henry promptly displayed on London Bridge as a warning to other people who might wish to oppose him.

Thomas' daughter Margaret, who had married into the Roper family, lived in Canterbury. She rescued her father's head and had it properly buried in the family tomb in St Dunstan's Church. The brick gateway to the Roper's house can still be seen today almost opposite. Later, in the 19th century, the Pope 'beatified' Thomas, one step short of being named a saint.

Thomas Cranmer, who was appointed Archbishop of Canterbury in 1533, became a great supporter of Henry's new Church of England. Along with Thomas Cromwell, Cranmer encouraged the translation of the Bible into English and also wrote prayers that are still used in Anglican churches today.

When Henry's daughter 'Bloody' Mary became Queen, catholicism was once again the official religion of the country and those who did not follow the faith were dealt with cruelly. More than 40 protestant martyrs were burned at the stake in a field in south Canterbury between 1555 and 1558. A stone cross and small garden in Martyr's Field Road mark the spot today.

After a long trial and imprisonment, Cranmer was forced by Queen Mary to proclaim his error in supporting protestantism. Despite this, he was sentenced to be burned to death in 1556.

When another of Henry's daughters – Elizabeth I – came to the throne in 1558 everything changed again. Elizabeth was a Protestant. She wanted England to have peace and not be divided over religion, so she tried to find agreement between the opposing catholic and protestant sides. Elizabeth did not call herself the Head of the Church of England, but the 'Supreme Governor of the English Church'.

There was also a lot of religious unrest on the Continent. Protestant Walloon and Huguenot families from France, Holland and Belgium were allowed to escape the persecution in their own countries and settle in Canterbury. Their main occupation was weaving and it is said that, at one time, there were more than 1,000 looms in the town, providing a welcome boost to the local economy.

With the town's new found prosperity and the honour of having the Queen's support, Canterbury would remember Elizabeth's golden reign with gratitude.

FOCUS ON: CHRISTOPHER MARLOWE – WRITER AND SPY!

Christopher (Kit) Marlowe was a famous Elizabethan poet and writer of plays who was born in Canterbury in 1564. The son of a shoemaker, Christopher attended The King's School and was awarded a scholarship to study theology at Cambridge. Whilst there, he took a break in his studies... some say to carry out a secret mission for the government!

Christopher may well have become a priest, but instead he went to London to write plays. There he made some important friends, including Sir Walter Raleigh, a favourite of the Queen. It seems he also made quite a few enemies!

In 1589 Christopher was charged with murder and sent to prison. He was released two weeks later. It would not be the last time the hot-headed writer had a brush with the law. In 1592 an injunction was brought against him because of a street fight in which a man died and Christopher was later deported from Holland for counterfeiting gold coins.

Christopher's plays had a huge influence on the theatre of his time. William Shakespeare was certainly inspired by his work. Some even say that some of Shakespeare's plays were actually written by Marlowe!

Christopher died in suspicious circumstances aged only 29, a week after a warrant had been issued for his arrest. He was stabbed in the head during a fight at a London tavern and buried two days later in an unmarked grave. His killer pleaded self-defence and received a pardon from the Queen.

Christopher's colourful career lasted only six years. He is remembered in the name of Canterbury's theatre – the Marlowe – and by a monument to the Muse which stands outside.

2

1

1 A page from *The tragicall history of the life and death of Doctor Faustus* by Ch. Mar. (i.e. Christopher Marlowe) published in 1620

2 A portrait believed to be of Marlowe as a young man, painted in 1585

3 *The Passionate Shepherd to His Love* by Marlowe – one of the most popular Elizabethan poems

3 Come live with me and be my Love,
And we will all the pleasures prove
That hills and valleys, dale and field,
And all the craggy mountains yield.
Will we sit upon the rocks
And see the shepherds feed their flocks,
By shallow rivers, to whose falls
Melodious birds sing madrigals.

INN EXCESS
A NEW KIND OF TOURIST

WHAT TO SEE & DO

The Westgate has stood for six centuries on guard over the road to and from London. It now houses a museum telling the story of the city's defences and the gate's use as a jail and police station.

Stroll along the city walls by Dane John Gardens. Climb up the mound for a great view of the city and the monument to Alderman James Simmons.

The coloured paving bricks in the High Street near Best Lane mark the spot of the former All Saint's Church.

DID YOU KNOW...?

Dr James Beaney became a very rich man during the 19th century Australian gold rush. He left £10,000 to Canterbury to build the Beaney Institute 'for the education of the labouring man'. It now houses the city's public library and Royal Museum.

Most of the gateways into the city were demolished during the 18th and 19th centuries, when a local Act was passed to repave and widen Canterbury's roads. Only one of the gates still stands today – Westgate – which was built in 1380 and used to house a drawbridge and portcullis. For a long time it was also the town's jail.

Better roads and access into the city led to a growth in stagecoach travel. Large inns were built to accommodate the stagecoaches, their passengers and horses on their way to and from London and the Channel ports. A ticket to London cost 18 shillings (90p) and it would take six hours to get there!

The most important inn was the George and Dragon, which was located in the High Street where the Beaney Institute stands today. At one point this inn was the stopping-off point for 19 different stagecoach companies! Other inns in the city included the Fountain in St Margaret's Street, the Queen's Head in Watling Street and Rose in Rose Lane. One day Queen Victoria stayed at the Fountain and shortly after its name changed... to the *Royal* Fountain Inn!

During the 19th century the popularity of stagecoach travel declined as the railways grew in importance and, in time, all the inns were demolished.

Canterbury's strategic location and proximity to the Continent attracted a different sort of visitor during the Napoleonic Wars. From 1794 to 1811, barracks to house 5,000 infantry, cavalry and artillery troops were built to the north of the city. Their location is now covered by housing estates, but Military Road and Artillery Street remind us of their existence.

Military bands played in the recently landscaped Dane John Gardens. Alderman James Simmons paid for the planting of the gardens and avenue of lime trees, as well as the restoration of the famous mound, originally a Roman burial and later the site of a Norman keep. His memorial now stands on top of it.

Alderman Simmons was not only a generous benefactor but also a very good businessman. He realised that the industry now growing up in and around the city needed a better way of transporting heavy goods to London. He hit upon the idea of widening and deepening the River Stour to create a canal between Canterbury and the sea at St Nicholas Bay or Sandwich. His dream never became a reality: it was steam not water power that won the day!

1 Replica of Napoleon's personal flintlock pistol, made in 1806 and carried by him in his overcoat

2 Stagecoach in Canterbury High Street outside the George and Dragon Inn – an engraving by Thomas Sidney Cooper

3 The Westgate tower, built in 1380, and the last remaining gate to the city

4 The Beaney Institute, located on the site of the former George and Dragon Inn

5 A memorial to Alderman James Simmons tops the Dane John mound

1

1. Coloured lithograph of the opening of the Canterbury & Whitstable Railway in 1830, viewed from the Tyler Hill tunnel entrance

2. A later locomotive emerges from the same tunnel, whose entrance can still be seen at the back of The Archbishop's School

3. A Victorian engraving of Canterbury West Station in 1846

4. The original *Invicta* steam engine, built by George and Robert Stephenson

5. Train ticket for the short journey between Whitstable Harbour station and Tankerton Halt

2

4

3

TUNNEL VISION
THE RAILWAY PIONEERS

On 3 May, 1830 an excited group of 300 rail passengers pulled into Whitstable Harbour station. They were the first people ever to use a regular passenger rail service. A six mile long single track now connected Canterbury with the coast.

The Crab & Winkle Line, as it became known, was a mammoth feat of engineering, yet it took just five years to build. Its main purpose was to transport coal, grain and other heavy goods. But it took passengers, too, and it was the first railway to offer season tickets – to take Canterbury residents to the seaside during the summer!

The line began at a small station in North Lane, Canterbury, and finished a few metres short of the harbour at Whitstable. Its route required the construction of a 764m long tunnel through Tyler Hill, as well as a road bridge in Whitstable, both world railway firsts.

Many of the country's leading engineers were involved in the line, including George and Robert Stephenson, Thomas Telford, Isambard Kingdom Brunel and William James.

A steam locomotive – the first one was called the *Invicta* – pulled the carriages for only a small part of the journey between Bogshole and South Street. It wasn't powerful enough to pull the carriages up the hills! For the rest of the journey, cables from steam winding engines were attached to the carriages to pull them up. Coming down the hills was left to gravity, with the carriages reaching speeds of up to 30 miles per hour. That must have seemed frighteningly fast for travellers more used to leg or horse power!

Sadly, the Crab & Winkle Line never made any money for its pioneering investors. The South-East Railway took it over in 1844 and a year later opened a new station – Canterbury West. The company ran the line until it was finally shut down in 1953, when many similar small branch lines were closed across the country.

At one point there were three stations serving the city – Canterbury West, East and South (located near where the Kent and Canterbury Hospital now stands).

During the second world war the Tyler Hill tunnel was used as an air raid shelter. In 1974 it was filled with concrete when part of the tunnel caved in under the weight of the university buildings above. Much of the line's route is now a cycle path.

WHAT TO SEE & DO

You can still see the railway tunnel entrances near The Archbishop's School and on the other side of the university at Tyler Hill.

Invicta once stood by the Riding Gate in Watling Street. It is now housed in the Museum of Canterbury.

Enjoy a picnic or a break from cycling at the winding engine pond in Clowes Wood between Blean and Tyler Hill.

DID YOU KNOW...?

With its plentiful supply of clay and wood for charcoal, Tyler Hill was a major centre of tile production during the 13th and 14th centuries.

A campaign is under way to extend the Canterbury to Whitstable cycle route and to reopen the tunnel.

BLITZED!
A CITY AT WAR

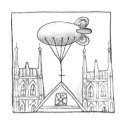

WHAT TO SEE & DO

The Museum of Canterbury houses a fascinating exhibit on the Second World War.

Visit Rupert Bear and his friends in their very own museum alongside. Rupert's creator, Mary Tourtel, lived and worked in the city.

The Spitfire & Hurricane Memorial Museum at Manston showcases these two classic RAF fighters. Displays alongside tell the story of the 'Battle of Britain' over Kent.

Early on in the Second World War the Royal Air Force launched a devastating bombing raid on the German cathedral city of Cologne. It set off a chain of events that would have far-reaching consequences for Canterbury and its citizens, both during and after the war.

In retaliation for the Cologne attack, Germany targeted strategically unimportant but picturesque cities in England... those that had been awarded three stars in the German Baedeker Travel Guide to Britain!

Canterbury was high up on this list of so-called 'Baedeker' targets. It should have come as no surprise, therefore, when the air raid warning sirens echoed around the city in the early hours of Monday, 1 June 1942. It was Canterbury's turn to receive a battering from Hitler's Luftwaffe.

Over the next 75 minutes, thousands of high explosives and incendiaries rained down on the city. Streets reverberated with the pounding of bombs, the roar of flames and crashing of collapsing buildings.

People huddled together in their underground shelters not knowing whether their homes would still be standing when they eventually emerged. An eerie red glow hung over Canterbury and people for miles around concluded that their beautiful cathedral city must have been destroyed.

Hundreds of firefighters from across Kent and even as far as London rushed to the city's aid. They set to work smothering the flames with water or creating fire breaks to prevent flames spreading to other buildings. Rescue parties worked tirelessly to dig people out from under the rubble of their collapsed homes.

Because of the inaccuracy of German bombers and the prompt action of the fire wardens manning its roof, the cathedral itself escaped largely unharmed. Its Victorian library, however, was destroyed. Fortunately the cathedral staff had had the good sense to remove the library's most precious contents to a safer location in the crypt at the outbreak of war.

By dawn, most of the main fires had been extinguished and the smaller ones had burned themselves out. Although many wooden Medieval buildings had been destroyed, it was actually the newer,

2

1. The Spitfire remains one of the best British fighter aircraft of all time

2. A devastated St George's Street in the aftermath of the June 1942 bombing raid

3. Marks and Spencer – miraculously the only shop left standing in St George's Street!

4. The wrecked St George's Church, whose clock tower is all that remains today

5. Alongside Westgate, school boys look on whilst soldiers prepare for a German invasion

6. (Overleaf) Rationing continued until well after the war

7. (Overleaf) Canterbury children as young as five were evacuated, mostly to Reading in Berkshire

3

4

5

Britain declared war on Germany on 3 September 1939. Within minutes the air raid siren sounded in Canterbury, warning of an imminent attack... it was a false alarm!

By early September 1940 most Canterbury children had been evacuated, as the city was no longer considered safe.

During 'blackouts' the lights on bikes, cars, buses and trains had to be masked and traffic lights hooded. This was to ensure that no lights could be seen from the air that might help guide enemy bombers.

During World War II, 445 high explosive bombs and an estimated 10,000 incendiaries fell on Canterbury.

The period immediately after the war was known as the 'buddleia years' as the flower flourished on bomb sites across the city.

Georgian area of the city – particularly around St George's Street, Burgate and The Parade – that had suffered most. In fact, the only building left completely standing in St George's Street was Marks and Spencer's! The tower of the nearby St George's church was all that remained of the building where Christopher Marlowe had been christened. It still stands today as a memorial to all those Canterbury citizens who lost their lives in the war – as St George's Clocktower.

Being a Monday morning many people made their way into the city as usual to find that their place of work no longer existed. All the roads in the centre of the city were closed to traffic and buses had to stop on the outskirts. Gas, water and electricity supplies were all cut off. Emergency centres were opened to provide food and shelter for people who had lost their homes. Over the coming months many shops would re-open – either by making hasty repairs, relocating to other parts of the city or sharing space with other businesses.

Fifty people were killed in the 1 June raid, including six children. But the death toll could have been much higher if the German bombs had not landed on the relatively empty business areas of the city.

Many people believed that the bombers would return that night to finish the

CHILDREN
are safer in the country
. . . leave them there

job. More anti-aircraft guns as well as barrage balloons, whose cables were designed to interfere with low flying aircraft, were installed in open spaces to defend the city.

The Luftwaffe did return, but not until 31 October. This time 20 German aircraft attacked the city in broad daylight as people went about their everyday business. Twenty high explosive bombs were dropped and city centre shoppers riddled with machine gun fire. Many people were injured as they dived for cover or were slashed by glass from shattering windows.

Apart from relatively minor incendiary and V1 rocket attacks in 1944 this was the last time that the city of Canterbury had to endure Hitler's wrath.

FOCUS ON: GHOSTLY GOINGS-ON!

Any historic city has its fair share of ghost stories and Canterbury is no exception!

Nell Cook, a cathedral canon's housekeeper, poisoned him and his mistress when she discovered their affair. She disappeared soon after, and many years later a woman's body was found under a pavement near the cathedral's Green Court. Nell's troubled ghost is said to haunt the nearby alleyways after midnight... but she is only seen by those who are soon to die themselves!

A woman called Abigail committed suicide after several years of being beaten by her husband. She ultimately had the last laugh, as her death was mistaken as murder. Soon after, her husband was found guilty and hanged. Abigail's spirit is said to haunt the upstairs of a building in Hawks Lane.

A phantom girl dressed in grey was seen to enter the front door of a building in St Margaret's Street and climb the staircase before vanishing. A skeleton was later discovered by builders under the floorboards, draped in grey cloth!

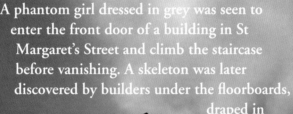

Builders working on another building in St Margaret's Street reported the sounds of children playing on the staircase, strange noises in the attic and youngsters whispering in a panelled room.

Spooky!

1 The entrance to Green Court by the cathedral

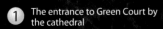
2 Hawks Lane runs between St Margaret's/Stour Street

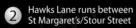
3 St Margaret's Street, scene of several reported hauntings!

Roman coins, dating from the second to fourth centuries

Roman copper alloy spoon, brooch, two cosmetic implements, tweezers and needle

Pottery from the second to fourth centuries, made in Kent and Oxfordshire

Roman glass bottle

Decorated bone comb, probably eighth century

Graffiti on a stone block from the Whitefriars friary, possibly from the monks' dormitory!

Lead document seal of Pope Nicholas V featuring the images of St Peter and St Paul, found at Whitefriars

Parchment fragments found in a shallow pit outside the Whitefriars friary

Fragment of stained glass, probably from a Whitefriars friary window

Pottery from the Whitefriars friary cess-tanks, probably dumped at the time of the Dissolution

Clay pipes from around 1600-1640

Glass medicine bottles, probably 18th century, which would have had cork stoppers

SHOPPERS' PARADISE
THE NEW WHITEFRIARS

The area of the city we know today as Whitefriars has probably changed most in the years since the war. It was once home to the Austin – or White – Friars, whose monastery was dissolved by Henry VIII in 1538. In later years, the Simon Langton Girls and Boys Grammar Schools were founded on the site, before moving to their present locations in the 1950s.

The Whitefriars area was largely destroyed during the wartime bombing raids and was gradually rebuilt, with a mix of shops, offices and a multi-storey car park. During the late 1980s, the City Council decided to replace the development with something more appropriate to its historic setting and the needs of modern shoppers.

A number of architects put forward ideas for the Whitefriars site. After much discussion and a public exhibition, work on the new shopping centre began in September 1999. It was completed six years later.

During the centre's construction, archaeologists from the Canterbury Archaeological Trust (CAT) undertook the largest city centre excavation ever seen in this country. Over 30 months, they carried out a series of excavations across the site, which became known as 'The Big Dig'.

As many as 70 archaeologists and volunteers worked on the site at any one time, digging down to pre-Roman levels. Their discoveries included parchment and stained glass fragments from the Medieval friary, a previously unknown Roman bastion alongside the city wall, a beautifully preserved stretch of Anglo-Saxon road and a hoard of 700 Roman bronze coins. The CAT team also uncovered a forgotten graveyard containing over 200 bodies, which were later reburied at Canterbury cemetery.

Thousands of objects are still being reviewed and catalogued, helping us to fill in the missing gaps in Canterbury's fascinating 2,000-year history.

WHAT TO SEE & DO

The archaeologists' work is celebrated in Whitefriars Square. Look out for the engravings on the paving slabs that represent their original site drawings.

A Roman bastion display can be found by the city wall near the bus station.

1 Archaeologists work on the Whitefriars church site, now home to Fenwick

ACKNOWLEDGEMENTS

I'm grateful to Alison Hurst at Canterbury Cathedral, Martin Crowther at the Museum of Canterbury and Marion Green from the Canterbury Archaeological Trust for checking the historical accuracy of the content. Thanks also to Andrew Savage from CAT and Craig Bowen at the museum for their assistance researching suitable images, and to Stewart Ross for his encouragement. I'm grateful to Dr Margaret Griffin, Julia Bell and Anne Ovenden, whose perspective as teachers was especially welcome. I'd also like to thank Peter Scutt at Whitefriars for supporting this guide's production. Finally, a big thank you to all the authors, past and present, who have been equally inspired to tell the Canterbury story and whose works provided me with invaluable source material. Their respective titles are listed in the bibliography on the right. Do read them if your appetite has been whetted!

TEACHERS' RESOURCE GUIDE

An accompanying teachers' guide is available for free download from www.OOTBShop.co.uk. This includes additional educational resources as well as ideas for classroom activities.

Additional copies of this book can also be purchased online at www.OOTBShop.co.uk, with discounts available for larger orders.

PHOTO CREDITS

BIBLIOGRAPHY

The Blitz of Canterbury by Paul Crampton. Published by Meresborough Books, 1989. ISBN 0948 193 441.

Canterbury, scenes from the past published by Pitkin Pictorials, 1990. ISBN 0 85372 475 X.

Canterbury, 2,000 years of history by Marjorie Lyle. Published by Tempus Publishing, 2008. ISBN 978 0 7524 1948 0.

The Canterbury & Whitstable Railway by Brian Hart. Published by Wild Swan Publications Limited, 1991. ISBN 0 906867 97 5.

The Illustrated Portrait of Canterbury by John Boyle. Published by Robert Hale Limited. ISBN 0-7090-3522-5.

Roman Canterbury, a journey into the past by Andy Harmsworth. Published by Canterbury Archaeological Trust, 1995. ISBN 1-870545-01-X.

St Augustine's Abbey published by English Heritage, 1997. ISBN 1 85074 669 9.

The Young Person's Guide to Canterbury Cathedral published by Canterbury Cathedral. ISBN 0 906211 58 1.